Canals
and Waterways

Christopher Pick

Macdonald Educational

Contents

How to use this book

First look at the contents page and see if the subject you are looking for is listed. For instance, if you want to find out about locks, you will see that **Locks** are on page 18. The index will tell you where and how many times a particular subject is listed. For instance, you will see that locks are also mentioned on pages 6, 10, 13, 14, 19, 20, 21, 24, 26, 41 and 43.

page

6 Why canals were built
The importance of linking rivers, and later factories and towns. Why British canals were narrower than those in Europe and America.

8 Early canals
How trade could not expand until canals were built. Attempts to improve river traffic. The Canal du Midi.

10 The canal age in Britain
The Industrial Revolution and the important part that canals played. How industry and canals depended on each other. The Bridgewater Canal.

12 How canals were planned
Who built and paid for canals. Planning canal routes. Opposition to new canals, and why. Canal buildings. Tolls.

14 Building canals
Contractors. Early canal routes. Navvies. How canals were made watertight.

16 The end of the canal age in Britain
The coming of the railways, and why they were so successful. The decline of British canals during the middle of the 19th century. Canal planning in Europe.

18 Locks
How locks work and how much water is needed. Flights and staircases. Economizer locks.

20 Water supply
Why water needs to be replaced and where the water comes from. Pumping stations. The problems caused by drought or flood.

22 Tunnels
How tunnels were built and the work of the navvies. 'Legging' boats through tunnels.

24 Aqueducts
Roman aqueducts, and why they were built. Why aqueducts were needed. How water was kept in. Advances in aqueduct engineering and repair.

26   Alternatives to locks
Inclined planes, lifts and water slopes.

28   Boats
Wooden narrow boats and canal horses. Steam boats. Push-tows and how much they can carry.

30   Canal families
How people lived on boats. Canal boat decoration.

32   Canal children
The daily life of a 19th century canal child. The difficulties of going to school and of making regular friends.

34   Freight
British canal cargoes. Cargoes in other countries. Barge-carrying systems (LASH, BACAT and SEABEE).

36   Modern European canals
The Trans-Europe Waterway. Canals in the Soviet Union, and how they are used by traffic from very distant countries.

38   Canals in North America
How natural waterways were linked so that the mid-West could be opened up. The importance of the Mississippi. The St Lawrence Seaway and how ocean-going ships can sail 3,747 kilometres inland.

40   Suez and Panama
The political importance of the Suez Canal. The Suez Crisis in 1956 and the 1967 Six-Day War. The Panama Canal and why it was difficult to build. The Panama locks.

42   The future of inland waterways
Leisure use of canals in Britain. How European and American canals are used. British waterways and their future.

44   Other books to read and places to visit

45   Index

Above: One of the last canal horses, pulling a goods barge on a British canal

Below: A typical country canal in Britain. It is now used for holidays and no longer for freight

Why canals were built

Canals are waterways built by man. Unlike rivers, which were formed naturally, canals were built along a planned route. Some rivers had always been used for trade. Many were canalized (made deeper and wider) so that they could then take bigger boats. Before canals were built, men had had to rely on natural waterways. Building canals through land was a major achievement.

Where the early canals were built

The most important early canal was the Canal du Midi in France, finished in 1681. But it was in Britain that canals were first developed on a large scale. From the 1750's onwards, British engineers began to build canals. At first these simply linked major rivers which may have been far apart. But the Industrial Revolution made it vital to link factories and towns as well. The new factories needed raw materials such as coal, iron and cotton, which the canals brought. They produced goods which the canals took away to be sold in other towns. Until they were eventually replaced by railways in the mid-nineteenth century, canals were very important for the trade of the nation.

Why British canals were narrow

One of the big differences between canals in Britain and Europe is that British canals were built by private companies. One of the main aims of these companies was to make a big profit. As a result, many locks and bridges were built as narrow as possible to save money. Canals themselves were usually six to nine metres wide. No-one realized that the canals would soon be far too small and that trying to save money like that was a serious mistake.

Canals in Europe and America

Most of these canals were built later, and the same mistakes were not made. In Europe, the state usually paid for new canals throughout the country. This helped national trade instead of local trade near one particular canal. These European canals became so important that when competition from railways increased in the mid-19th century, they continued to flourish, though in Britain railways very quickly became more important than canals.

There is now a complete modern waterways system which carries about 25 per cent of Western Europe's trade, though in some countries much more.

Above: A busy canal quayside at the beginning of the 18th century

Below: Large grain-carrying ships moored on the Welland Canal in Canada, which can take huge ships with heavy and important cargoes

Early canals

Canals were the first way of travelling easily to all parts of the country. Before they were built, goods could only be moved along natural rivers or by packhorses along roads full of holes. Often, rivers were not deep enough to take even small boats. Usually, they did not go to the right part of the country.

Why trade could not expand

Trade on a large national scale, as we have today, was impossible before canals were built. It was difficult to carry raw materials, food and manufactured goods. Because coal, for example, was heavy and therefore expensive to transport, relatively little was produced until it was needed by the new factories. In many areas charcoal was burnt instead. Most people in villages and towns ate locally grown food and used locally made goods unless they were on the banks of a major river.

River navigation

Long before the first canals were built, attempts had been made to improve river traffic. Rivers were straightened and deepened. Locks were introduced so that boats could bypass changes in water level and waterfalls. In 1660, there were 1,055 kilometres of river navigation in Britain. By 1724, the number had increased to 1,856.

The Canal du Midi

In Europe too, similar improvements were being made. The Canal du Midi, which ran from the Atlantic to the Mediterranean, was completed 80 years before the Duke of Bridgewater's famous canal was built in Britain in 1761. Unlike canals in Britain, however, the Canal du Midi was not built to make it easier to transport goods. It was built because an inland route from the Atlantic to the Mediterranean was needed. This meant that ships could avoid the long and dangerous journey round the Straits of Gibraltar.

The Canal du Midi was built mostly with money given by the state. It is 240 kilometres long, 206 metres high and 16 metres wide. At the highest point it reaches, the summit level, an enormous dam was constructed to supply it with water. This was a spectacular engineering achievement. The canal also included the first staircase locks and the first canal tunnel at Malpas.

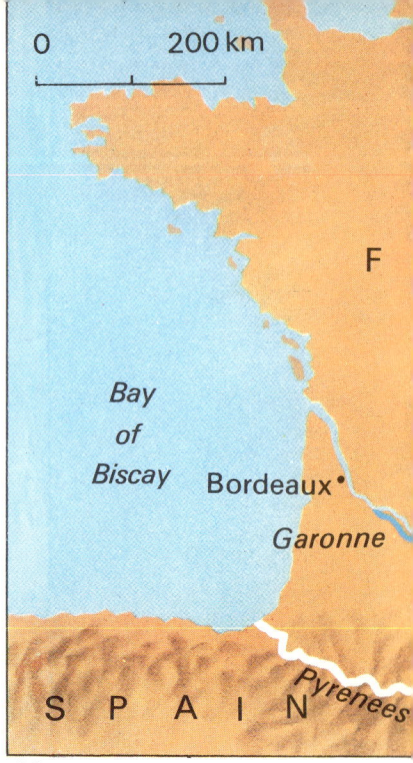

Above: A map showing the route of the Canal du Midi, finished in 1681. It is still used today

Paris

R A N C E

Lyons

Massif Central

Rhône

Avignon

Toulouse

Marseilles

Aude

Mediterranean
Sea

Pierre-Paul Riquet

The building of the Canal du Midi was a landmark in canal engineering. It was also the first canal big enough to take ships as well as boats. Pierre Paul Riquet, who worked on it for 14 years, became known throughout France.

There were very many problems during the construction of the canal. The work took much longer than the engineers had estimated. It was also very expensive. At one time, there were 12,000 people, including 600 women, working at digging and building. But a lot of people thought that Riquet was spending far too much of the state's money. They didn't believe that the canal would ever be finished and that the money would be wasted. When the French government refused to give him any more money, Riquet was so determined to finish the work that he paid for it himself. He died in 1680, heavily in debt, a year before the canal was opened.

Below: During the 18th century, travel was difficult because the roads were so bad. Carrying goods by river was quicker and more reliable

The canal age in Britain

The period between about 1760 and 1840 was the great canal age in Britain. In this quite short time, a dense network of over 6,400 kilometres of canal was built, criss-crossing the countryside. Eventually, no important town was more than about 15 kilometres from a waterway. Large industrial towns frequently had canals running through them. Even today, Birmingham has more canals than Venice!

The Industrial Revolution

It is not a coincidence that the Industrial Revolution was happening at the same time as the expansion of the canals. In the eighty years between 1760 and 1840, Britain stopped being an agricultural nation with a few small industries supplying mainly local needs. Instead, it was becoming a country of smoking factories and big industrial towns. Goods were being sent out not only all over Britain but also to much of the world. Ports had to become larger to handle the goods that were exported.

Above: An 18th century river barge

Below: These two maps show how many canals were built in Britain between 1760 and 1840

1760

1840

Navigable rivers
Canals
0   150 km

The canals in Britain played a tremendously important part in the development of the Industrial Revolution. Raw materials, for instance coal and iron, had to be sent from one region to another. Finished goods had to be delivered to the big cities and then to the docks. Without canals, this would have been impossible.

Canals helped industry and trade to grow. The process also happened the other way round. Because industry was growing and more goods were being made, there was a need for better and improved transport. The canals met this need. So industry and trade made canal development important and successful.

The Bridgewater Canal

The Bridgewater Canal (the first to be built in Britain) was finished in 1761. It was named after the Duke of Bridgewater, who planned it and who paid for it. It was 16.8 kilometres long and also included an aqueduct over the river Irwell at Barton. This was the first aqueduct that boats could sail along in Britain. The canal was originally built to carry coal from the mines on the Duke's estate at Worsley to Manchester, which was then quite a small town.

The Bridgewater Canal made the Duke rich. James Brindley, the engineer who worked with the Duke, became very famous, and Manchester became one of Britain's leading industrial towns.

The plan that Brindley then worked out to link the chief rivers of England was extremely important. The Severn and the Mersey were connected in 1771. The Trent was joined to them in 1777, five years after Brindley's death.

'Canal mania'

After the success of the Bridgewater Canal, more and more canals were built to supply the increasing needs of the new factories. The most important ones covered the industrial Midlands, the route across the Pennines, the direct routes from the Midlands to London, and the western route via the Thames to Bristol. Anyone who thought he might make money out of building a canal became enthusiastic about them. A large number of canal companies were started. This 'canal mania' continued until the first railways were built in the 1830's.

Above: Men deepening a canalized river during the early 18th century

Below: Francis, Duke of Bridgewater with his canal and aqueduct

How canals were planned

Unlike the Bridgewater Canal, most canals were not built and paid for by a single rich man. Usually a group of men who were perhaps landowners, factory-owners, merchants or lawyers, got together to build a canal in a particular district. They hoped it would improve trade and travel in the area and make a good profit.

Planning the route

Before the canal could be built, a route had to be planned. Then the company had to get a Bill through Parliament allowing them to go ahead with their plans. Professional engineers did the survey which decided where the canal should go. The most famous of these were Brindley, Thomas Telford and William

Above: Navvies digging out the bed of a new canal. You can see the rope and stakes that marked the canal route

Below: Canal engineers in the 18th century deciding where a new canal should go

Jessop. The engineers explored the area to find the best route for the canal.

Opposition to new canals

When the Bill came to be discussed in Parliament, there were often a lot of objections. Millowners were afraid that their mills might lose water. The farmers, whose corn was ground in the mills, also protested. People concerned with road transport or coastal shipping were frightened of competition from the canals.

Land for new canals could only be bought, and work begin, if the Bill was accepted. Even then, the company's troubles were still not always over. Often there were unexpected difficulties and delays. Sometimes, the company went bankrupt, and the canal was left unfinished.

Canal buildings

As well as the canal itself, bridges, lock-keeper's cottages, warehouses, stables and workshops had to be built by the company. A lot of these buildings can still be seen beside canals today.

Tolls

The company's work was not over even when the canal was finished. Payments called tolls had to be fixed for the boats that used the canals. This money was very important. Since it was the main source of income for the company, a toll could not be fixed too low because no profit would be made. If tolls were too high, boats would use rival canals. In addition, the canal itself had to be kept repaired. An engineer was usually employed to do this. He was helped by lock-keepers and men called lengthsmen, who walked along the tow-paths checking the water level in the canal.

Above: Bridges like these let a canal horse cross the canal without being untied

Above: An 18th century warehouse by a canal

Below: An 18th century lock-keeper's cottage in Britain

Building canals

When a company was ready to build its canal, the first stage was to peg out the actual line. This meant that the engineer (or, more probably, one of his assistants) rode over the whole route, marking out the exact path that the canal would take with rope and stakes.

Contractors

At the same time, the company hired a firm of contractors who were responsible for the actual construction. This firm in turn hired the workmen who did the hard physical labour. Often there were disagreements between the canal company and the contractors. The most common complaints were about payment and the quality of the work. Contractors often worked on several canals in different parts of the country and tended not to bother to follow the engineer's instructions. Sometimes, they went bankrupt and simply disappeared.

Early canal routes

The first canals followed the lie of the land. Whenever possible, they went round hills rather than underneath them. This was partly because no-one yet had much experience of digging tunnels or cuttings. Such work was also very expensive. In addition, the more places a canal served, the more opportunities there were for business. A longer route was not necessarily a bad thing.

By the 1820's and 1830's engineering knowledge had increased, and canals were built straight across country, following the fastest and most direct route. In hilly country, staircase locks or enormous cuttings, embankments or aqueducts were constructed.

Above: James Brindley (1716-1772), a famous British canal builder

Below: Thomas Telford (1757-1834), who also built roads and railways

Navvies

At first, most of the people who built the canals were local men. As more and more canals were built, gangs of men teamed up and moved from one canal to another, rather as labourers do today on new motorways. In the 1790's about 50,000 men were working on canals all over the country. The word 'navvy' (short for 'navigator') was first used to describe these canal workmen. The navvies' work was hard, tiring and often dangerous. They had to dig out the earth with a pick and shovel and wheel it away on a barrow. Once some of the canal had been completed, water could be let in from nearby streams or rivers and then boats were used to take the rest of the earth away.

'Puddling'

Before water could be let in, the canal had to be made waterproof. This was done by 'puddling'. The 'puddle' was a mixture of loam and clay. When it was spread on the bottom and sides of the canal and trampled down to a thickness of about 30 centimetres, it formed a watertight seal. It was both simple and effective. Most canals have remained intact since the puddle was first laid.

Accidents during canal construction were frequent and there was rarely any medical help. The navvies were often paid only in 'token' money, which had to be spent in shops owned by the canal company. Drunkenness and stealing were quite common. Because of this, the local villagers sometimes dreaded the arrival of the canal-builders. Once the canal was open, however, canal-side towns, shops and villages became much more prosperous.

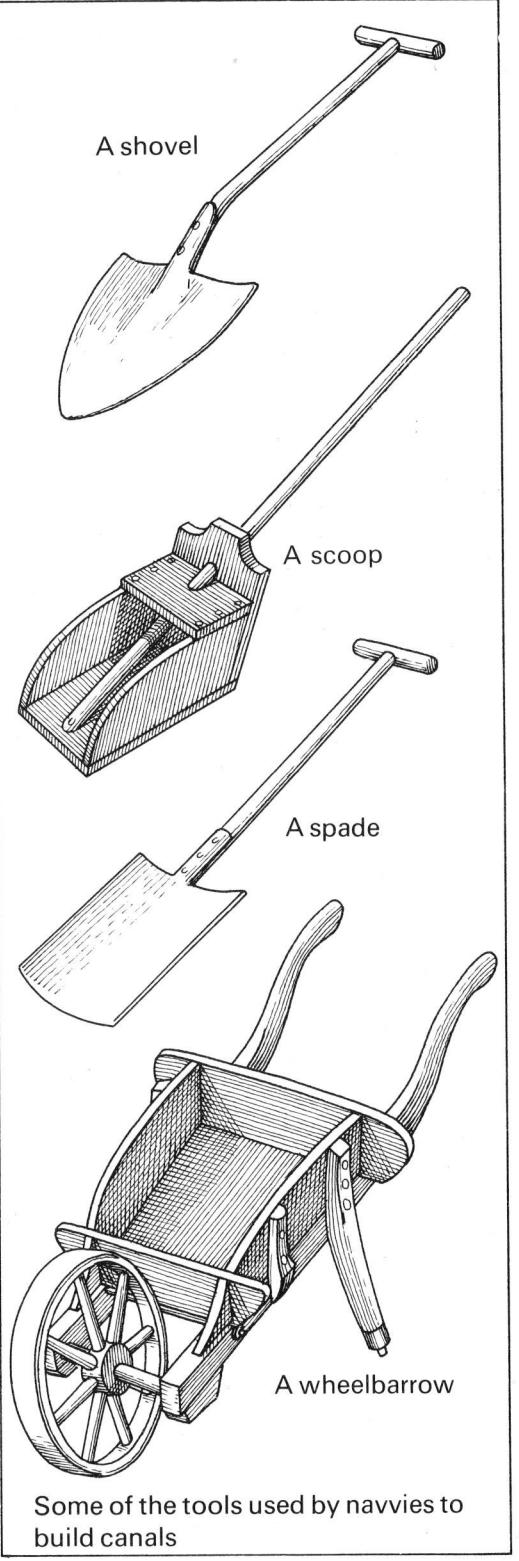

A shovel

A scoop

A spade

A wheelbarrow

Some of the tools used by navvies to build canals

The end of the canal age in Britain

The growth of railways in the mid-19th century meant that sooner or later canals would become less important. Trains were quicker, more comfortable and could carry more goods than canals. Some canal companies were quickly bought up by railways so as to prevent competition. Others survived, but most were never as profitable again.

Why railways were so successful

From the start, railway engineers used the knowledge and experience in construction that had been gained during the building of the canals. This meant that railways ran efficiently and a lot of basic mistakes in planning were not made. Trains were much quicker than canals. It took several days to reach Birmingham from London by canal but only a few hours by train. Railways were also cheaper. They attracted a lot of passengers and so the overhead running costs (the money needed for wages, repairs and equipment) could be paid for by passenger fares. This meant, therefore, that goods could be carried more cheaply than on the canals.

The decline of British canals

Most canals were now far too small. Narrow boats could only carry between 20 and 25 tonnes of goods at the most. A train could carry far more, and to far more parts of the country. From about the middle of the 19th century onwards, canals became less and less profitable. Some shut completely. Others kept a few regular customers, but rarely gained new ones.

Above: Canals were very busy until the railway network covered the whole country

Below: A ship being guided by a tug along the Manchester Ship Canal. The Barton Aqueduct, which runs over the Ship Canal, has been swung to the centre to let the ship pass through

At the end of the 19th century, there were hopes in Britain of a revival. The Manchester Ship Canal, which made Manchester a major sea-going port, was opened in 1894. But other plans, for instance to connect Birmingham with the sea, came to nothing. The state eventually took control of almost all canals in 1948.

Canal planning in Europe

In Europe, canals had been looked after by the state rather than by private companies since the end of the 19th century. An enormous programme of canal improvement was started. In France, the canals linking three main rivers—the Seine, the Rhône and the Rhine—were rebuilt between 1880 and 1900 and larger locks were built. In Germany, the Dortmund-Ems canal, opened in 1899, connected the country's most industrial region with the sea at Emden, 165 kilometres to the north. In this century, new canals have been opened in Europe and old ones deepened to take bigger traffic. As a result, the busy inland waterways of Europe play a very important part in trans-continental transport.

Above: Large barges on the River Rhine in Germany. This is one of the main water routes in Europe

Below: This scene in west London shows a canal, motorway and railway running almost side by side

Locks

Locks are the most important part of the canal system. They are like steps in a staircase which take boats up or down hill, so that they can travel where river traffic cannot.

How locks work

The way in which a lock works is very simple and is usually the same everywhere. In Britain, locks are usually hand-operated, whereas on all important commercial canals electric power is used. The lock itself is a kind of box with gates at each end. The gates have sluices in them which open and close to control the flow of water.

Going up

If a boat is going up hill, it enters the lock, the bottom gates are shut and the sluices on the top gates are opened so that water flows in. When the water in the lock reaches the same level as the canal above, the sluices are shut, the gates are opened and the boat continues on its journey.

Going down

If the boat is going down hill, it goes straight into a full lock, the bottom sluices are opened, and the water flows out. When the water level in the lock sinks to that of the canal below, the boat can go on.

A boat travelling up hill will often arrive at a lock and find that it is full, or one going down may come to an empty one. Then, it has to wait while the lock is emptied or filled specially. All this takes about 10 minutes on a narrow canal.

Locks and water

Locks use up an enormous amount of water. An average narrow lock holds between 113,000 and 136,000 litres.

Above: The famous staircase locks at Bingley, in Britain. Five broad locks run directly together and it can take nearly an hour for a boat to pass through them

Below: This is what you see when you look down into an unfilled lock. The difference between the two levels is quite clear

When there is a water shortage, locks are often worked in alternate directions. This means that if a boat going up hill arrives at a full lock, it has to wait until a boat has passed through in the other direction.

Side ponds

Side ponds are another way of saving water. They are built at the side of the lock and are linked to it by a channel. When a lock is emptied, half the water flows into the side pond, so that it fills up completely. It is only then that the sluices on the bottom gates are opened to let the rest of the water out.

When a boat comes up hill, the side pond is emptied into the lock first. The top sluices are opened afterwards. In this way, only half as much water as usual is used.

Flights and staircases

In very hilly areas, one lock after another may be needed. These series of locks are called flights or staircases. Flights are groups of locks with fairly short stretches of water between them. Sometimes, there may be as many as 30 within a few kilometres.

Staircases look very dramatic. The bottom gates of one lock are also the top gates of the next one going down. A long wait is often necessary before taking a boat through a staircase. If the locks are full and the boat is travelling up hill, all the locks have to be emptied. The bottom one is emptied first, then the second into the bottom, and so on.

Economizer locks

On many European canals, 'economizer' locks are used. These work like ordinary locks, except that they are very much larger and can take far bigger boats, which saves water.

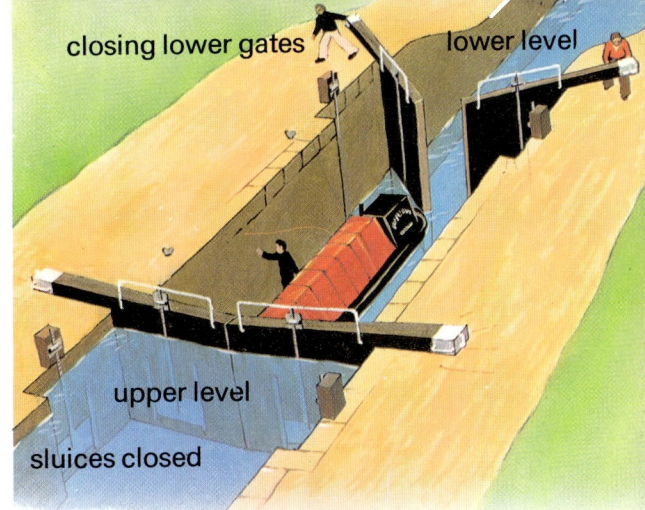

Above: The barge enters the lock and the gates are closed behind it

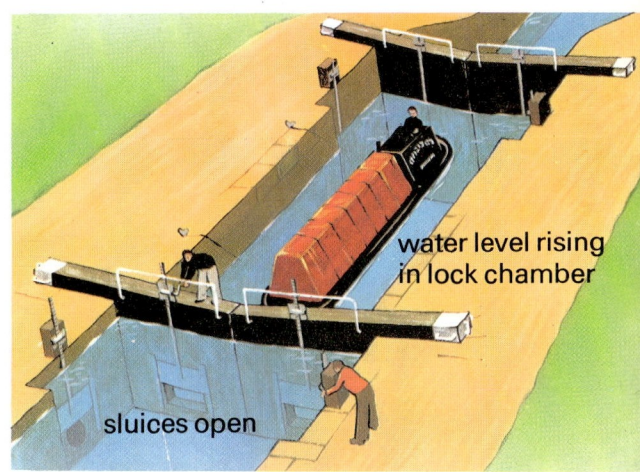

Above: The sluices have been opened and the barge is rising as water fills the lock

Below: Now that the lock is full, the gates are opened and the barge can continue on its journey

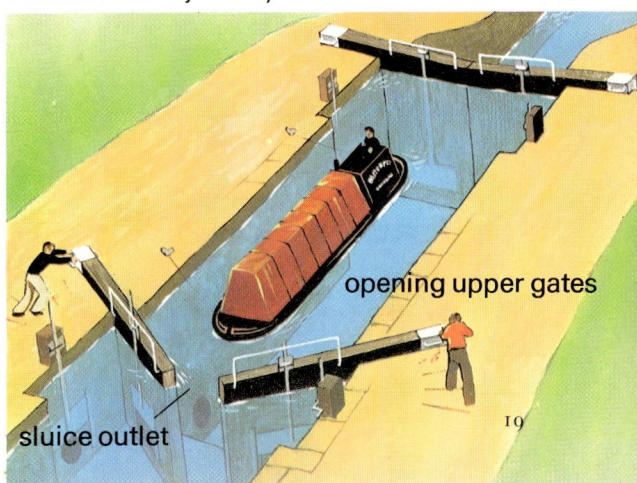

19

Water supply

As a boat climbs towards the summit level (or highest level) of a canal, it uses one lock-full of water. In the same way, as it travels down from the summit level, it also takes the equivalent of a lock-full of water with it, although whichever way the boat is travelling the water always goes downhill. This water must be replaced. If it is not, the canal would very quickly dry up.

Where the water comes from

Most water for canals comes from streams and small rivers. Sometimes, these flow directly into the canal. More often, they are diverted into catchment reservoirs. These are connected with the canal by a narrow feeder channel. Water is then let into the canal whenever necessary. Some canals also get water from storage reservoirs in which rain-water is collected.

Pumping stations

Pumping stations were built on canals if water was not available at the summit level, or if more water was needed. These are now worked by diesel oil or electricity, though at first they were steam operated. They lift water from rivers and reservoirs at a lower level and sometimes from underground streams. They also bring back water from locks lower down the canal so that it can be used again.

Other sources of water

Even if the summit level is well supplied with water, there can still be problems of supply. This is because not all boats travel right up to the summit level, and the water they use has to be replaced lower down. If a second canal branches off, it takes a great deal of water. Factories on or near the

Above: Badly polluted water in a canal near a factory. Most factories now have to clean dirty water before it is allowed to run into a canal

Below: A canal bank that has burst. You can see that a lot of water has flowed away so that the canal bed is exposed

canal also use a lot. Pounds (stretches of water between locks) which are at a lower level sometimes have to be supplied by reservoirs. In a low-lying area, a river may be used to keep a canal supplied with water.

Droughts and floods

The worst problems for people in charge of canals are droughts and floods. In very hot weather, some water evaporates, especially from long pounds. Even the normal sources of water may be reduced or occasionally dry up altogether. If just one part of the canal is affected, water can be let down through locks or through the weirs beside them. If the drought gets more serious, use of the canal may have to be limited or even stopped completely.

In wet weather, water can be let out of the canal either by sending it down through the locks and out of the canal entirely or by opening special channels which lead into nearby streams and rivers. Checking that the banks are not in danger of breaking is a very important job when there are floods. In towns, canals are often used to drain excess water from roads and buildings and then to store it or send it where it is needed.

How canal water is used

In industrial areas, canals provide a great deal of water for nearby factories and power stations. Most of it is used for cooling machinery and is then returned to the canal. Very little is wasted.

Today, there are strict rules to prevent water pollution. This is because until recently, dirty water from factories was simply let out into the canal. This was dangerous, as well as unpleasant. Nowadays, the water is cleaned or filtered before it runs back into the canal.

Above: This is what sometimes happens to a canal during a long drought. It may be months before boats can use the canal and lock

Below: A canal bank has burst and left a barge marooned in the mud. Water will have to be diverted from rivers and streams to fill the canal again

Tunnels

Tunnels were one of the most difficult parts of a canal to build. Engineers and canal companies tried to avoid building them whenever possible. All kinds of things could go wrong. The roof might fall in while the tunnel was being dug, trapping people. There were frequent falls and deaths from drowning. Tunnels were usually started from both ends at the same time, and it was therefore easy to miscalculate. Sometimes two parts of the tunnel did not join up.

How tunnels were built

First of all, a straight line was marked out over the top of the hill. Then a number of shafts (very deep holes), were sunk into the ground down to the level of the canal.

Above: Legging a barge loaded with timber through a tunnel

Below: A ventilation shaft built above a canal tunnel

Each shaft was about 150 metres apart. The navvies worked at the bottom of the shafts in each direction, digging the tunnel out with their bare hands and with simple tools. The earth was taken up the shafts and dumped on the ground, forming hillocks which can often still be seen. The navvies got fresh air through the shafts. Some of the shafts on British canals are still used for ventilation.

Legging

Because tunnels were so difficult to build, most tunnels had no towpaths. The boatmen had to find a way of getting their boats through the tunnels without a horse. The way they did this was by 'legging' the boats through while the horses were walked over the top, in the open air. Two crew members lay on their backs on boards sticking out sideways from the fore-end of the boat. The men pushed the boat through the tunnel by moving their feet along the walls and gripping the board tightly with their hands. Falls overboard were frequent, especially in wider tunnels.

'Leggers'

At some tunnels, groups of strong men earned their living by legging boats through the tunnel. They were known as 'leggers'. At Blisworth, on the Grand Union Canal, leggers were paid the equivalent of $7\frac{1}{2}$p a trip, for a journey of 2,794 metres. After 1870, full-time leggers were replaced by steam tugs. The steam these produced caused ventilation problems. The fumes from diesel boats later on made the situation worse. On several occasions, boatmen were suffocated and in some tunnels, old shafts had to be opened up to provide extra air.

Above: Building a canal tunnel at the beginning of the 19th century. Trucks were pushed along the rails to carry the earth and rocks away

Aqueducts

The Romans built the first aqueducts, 1,500 years before the canal age. Two of the most famous early aqueducts are the Pont du Gard, in southern France, and the one at Segovia, in Span. Roman aqueducts were built to bring water to towns and cities however, and not to carry boats.

Like tunnels, aqueducts are a way of taking a canal across a change of level, usually a river or a deep gorge. They were needed especially where a series of locks would have been difficult to build and then slow to travel through. People laughed when the idea of a navigable aqueduct was first suggested because the engineering problems seemed enormous.

How water was kept in

One of the main engineering problems was how to hold the water in. The first aqueduct built in Britain in 1761 at Barton, on the Bridgewater Canal, was made of stone. The water ran in a channel of earth and puddled clay.

The big advance in aqueduct engineering came when it was discovered that water could be held in cast-iron troughs. The troughs were light, and so the stone arches which carried the weight of the aqueduct could be built higher and narrower than before. The iron plates were bolted together and the joints sealed to keep the water in. The first aqueduct in Britain built in this new way was finished in 1795. In 1805, the aqueduct at Pontcysyllte in Wales was opened. It carried the Llangollen Canal over the River Dee and is still thought to be one of the most spectacular aqueducts in the world. It is 36 metres high and has 19 arches, each with a span of 13 metres. It was built by Jessop and Telford, two of the most famous canal engineers.

How aqueducts are repaired

Whether they are built of stone or iron or of steel and reinforced concrete (as today), aqueducts must be carefully maintained. The greatest danger is cold weather. If thick ice forms in the trough, it expands. This causes cracks in the structure of the aqueduct. In especially cold weather, the aqueduct can be sealed off from the rest of the canal by planks at each end. This is also done if any

Above: Sailing a boat across the Pontcysyllte Aqueduct. The towpath is protected by a railing, but on the other side there is a sheer drop

repairs are necessary. The water in the troughs can be released by pulling out a series of plugs, rather like giant bath plugs. It then crashes down into the valley below.

The modern Barton Aqueduct, which replaced Brindley's when the Manchester Ship Canal was built, consists of a huge tank, which can hold 800 tonnes of water. It can swing to one side from the centre when large ships need to pass underneath. Parallel gates are closed across each end of the tank to hold the water in. This means that the water need not be emptied out or diverted somewhere else each time the aqueduct has to be moved.

Below: The Pontcysyllte Aqueduct soon after it was built. A horse is pulling a barge across it

Alternatives to locks

A boat takes quite a long time to pass through a lock and also uses a lot of water. Because of this, canal-builders sometimes tried to think of different ways of by-passing locks, especially in hilly country where a large number of locks, one after the other, were necessary.

Inclined planes

Inclined planes are like simple railways, except that they carry boats, not carriages. One of the first to be built was the Hay incline, at Ironbridge, which linked the Shropshire Canal with the River Severn. It had two rails. Each rail carried a platform known as a cradle. The cradles were attached to a rope which was pulled by an engine. When a boat wanted to travel up or down the plane, it was loaded on to the cradle at the top and hauled down the slope. The other cradle and its boat acted as a balance and passed it halfway.

It took four men to work the plane, which could carry a pair of five or six tonne boats in $3\frac{1}{2}$ minutes. For the same distance, 27 ordinary locks would have been needed, and the journey would have taken two hours.

During the 19th century, a large number of inclined planes were also built in the United States. Modern inclined planes work in a similar way. However, they are operated by electricity and can take much larger loads.

Ronquières

One of the most modern inclined planes in Europe is at Ronquières, in Belgium. It can take barges carrying 1,350 tonnes over a slope of 1,430 metres. This avoids

Above: A diagram of the Anderton lift in operation. While the barges are being lowered in the tank, the balancing weights are moving up

Below: Three different views of an 18th century inclined plane. This one used water power to haul the boats up

a change of level of 68 metres. Before it was finished in 1968, 17 locks were needed to carry barges over the same distance.

Lifts

Like inclined planes, lifts can move boats quickly up or down a considerable height. Unlike them, however, the boats are not taken out of the water. Instead, they stay in a metal tank, which is lifted vertically from one level to another. Each end of the tank is sealed tightly by gates.

The first modern lift built was the Anderton Lift, which joined the Trent and Mersey Canal to the Weaver Navigation, 15 metres below. When it was opened in 1875 it was driven by steam, but in 1908 it was converted to electricity.

One of the newest lifts is on the Elbe Lateral Canal at Lüneberg in northern Germany. It was finished in 1975. It operates in the same way as the Anderton Lift, though it can take barges of up to 1,350 tonnes and lifts them 38 metres in only six minutes.

Water slopes

The water slope is the latest idea for moving boats from one level to another. It was developed by a French engineer at Montech on the Canal lateral à la Garonne. The slope by-passes five locks which take a boat down 13.30 metres within two kilometres.

The slope is operated by a diesel locomotive which runs beside the concrete slope. The boat itself travels in a triangular wedge of water which it enters at the top or bottom of the slope. The water is kept in by a shield made out of stainless steel. The whole journey takes six minutes and the boat travels at 5 kilometres an hour.

Above: A modern lift on a canal at La Louvière, in Belgium

Above: A modern inclined plane in Belgium. The tanks, which only carry one barge at a time, are balanced by weights running through the centre trough

Boats

Before the canals were built, a lot of different boats were used for coastal traffic and on the navigable rivers inland. In each different area boats were designed to suit the needs of local factories and industries.

Canal horses

Wooden narrow boats pulled by horses were the standard craft. Boats of a similar design are still in use today. After 1870 they were usually made of iron or steel instead of wood. They were 21 metres long, 2 metres wide and could carry up to 25 tonnes.

For nearly a century, all canal boats in Britain were pulled by horses. They walked slowly and steadily along the towpath, wearing pads to prevent the ropes rubbing and perhaps ear-caps in summer, to keep off the flies. A canal horse soon became used to its life and could be left to walk on its own safely. Occasionally, a horse would fall in to the water. Ramps can still be seen on some canals; these were used for hauling the horse back on to the towpath again.

Steam boats

In the 1860's, the first steam boats appeared on the canals. These were not very popular, mainly because the boilers and coal took up space that could otherwise have been filled by cargo. It was only when diesel engines were introduced in about 1910 that the horse was really threatened. The engines took up very little extra space and were cheap and easy to run. By the 1950's, commercial horse-drawn boats had completely disappeared.

Narrow boats were not the only craft to be seen on the British canals, however.

Above: A working canal horse, feeding as it walks along

Below: A pair of traditional working narrow boats on a British canal

Wide boats operated on the broader canals. These were often 21 metres long, like the narrow boats, and up to 4 metres wide.

American and European boats

Because the American and European canal networks were built later than the British system, they can take larger boats which carry larger loads. In Britain, most of the widest waterways can only take ships of up to 600 tonnes. In Europe, barges up to 100 metres long and 11.4 metres wide are frequent. They can take loads of up to 3,000 tonnes, though loads of 1,350 tonnes are more frequent. These larger barges are often built to take just one type of cargo—maybe oil, wine, grain, or even cars.

Push-tows

Another idea that has been developed recently (though it was first thought of as long ago as the mid-19th century) is the push-tow system. In this system, a number of wide barges, which are known as lighters, are lashed tightly together. They are then pushed by a tug, which sometimes has as many as three propellers and four rudders.

In Europe, push-tows usually consist of two to four lighters, carrying between 500 and 8,000 tonnes, though it is likely that up to 15,000 tonnes, on six lighters, will soon be common. On the Mississippi, by contrast, as much as 60,000 tonnes is moved by one push-tow.

One big advantage of the push-tow system is that the tug that pushes the lighters can be detached, rather like an engine from railway coaches. This means that the tug does not have to waste time waiting while the lighters are unloaded. Instead, it can immediately be attached to other lighters.

Below: Three push-tow barges going through industrial country in Britain

Canal families

From the 1840's onwards, most narrow boats in Britain were run by a family whose home was on the boat. Their life was rather a lonely one. It was rare for the children to go to school, and the family normally met only other boat families.

The first canal boats were worked by men only, or by men and boys. Some had helped to build the canals and then stayed on. Others lived in villages nearby and were glad to have a new source of work. Often, men came specially to look for work from places farther away. (For many years, people thought that the first boatmen were gypsies, but this is not true.) Until the 1840's, the boatman's family lived on land, usually near the canal. Then, increasing competition from the railways made the canal companies cut their wages. To save on rent, families moved on to the boats, even though it was sometimes difficult to fit a large family in to a small boat. All the family acted as crew and helped to look after the boat and horse.

Above: Children on a 19th century horse-drawn barge, moored by the canal bank while the horse has a rest

Below: The Keeshond, or Dutch Barge Dog, which was originally bred in Holland to live on barges and guard them at night

It was only after boats became family homes that they began to be decorated with the famous patterns of roses and castles. The roses and castles have no special meaning. They were just popular at the time and have been kept on ever since. They were also used to decorate water cans and dippers.

Above: A heavily-laden diesel boat just before the First World War

Earning a living

Earning a living on a canal was hard. Wages were very low. Boatmen were not paid by the hour but by each tonne of cargo delivered, so if they were held up through no fault of their own, they lost a lot of money. (Canals were sometimes frozen over for weeks in winter or closed for repairs.) Boatmen worked twelve to fifteen hours a day, seven days a week. The sooner a journey was finished, the sooner the boatman was paid and then his family could eat. If a boatman did about 40 seven day trips a year, he would earn a reasonable wage. This hardly ever happened.

After work was over in the evening, there was little to do except drink and talk or sing. Few boatmen ever learnt to read.

Above: Roses and castles were a favourite decoration

Above: A typical painted water can and dipper

Canal children

Canal families worked hard for little money in all kinds of weather. They also lived in very cramped conditions. Everything—cooking, eating, sleeping and washing—took place in one small cabin, although families often worked a pair of boats and therefore had two cabins.

Everyday life

If you had been a canal child in the second half of the 19th century, you would probably have been born on board, without any help from a doctor. A few days later, your father would have started up the boat again. Your parents and brothers and sisters would have looked after you when they had time, between chores. Within a couple of years, you would be sitting on the cabin roof, secured by a safety strap and harness. Your meals were

Above: Tea-time inside a barge during the late 19th century. The table folded back into the wall when it was not being used, to give everyone more room

Below: A pair of narrow boats still used for carrying coal

cooked on the wood or coal stove that also heated the cabin. You washed in the cabin, using a dipper (a metal hand bowl) in which crockery and clothes were also washed. The lavatory was an iron bucket which was emptied over the side when full. There was very little privacy.

By the time you were five, you would start helping to steer the boat and to feed and groom the horse, who usually got more attention than you did. Sometimes, you might go to school, though most canal children never did. At the end of the day, you might finish school and find that the boat had loaded up and moved on up the canal without you. That meant a walk of several miles to catch up with it!

Food was generally bought in shops near the canal and fishing and poaching helped to vary the diet a little. A few litres of water were carried in cans on the cabin roof, filled up at canalside taps. It was often easier, though, to take water for washing straight from the canal, using a dipper.

Social life

You would have lived a lonely life on the canals, with most of your time taken up helping on the boat. If you made friends with any other boat families, you would only see them every few weeks. Making friends was therefore rather difficult. When you did get married, a big family party was held, probably in a pub beside the canal. Early next morning, everyone would move off again, for honeymoons were unknown.

Boat people rarely left the canals. When they became too old to go on working, they moved to a cottage beside the canal or on to one of their children's boats.

Above: A corner of a barge cabin as it was 100 years ago. The kettle is heated by a wood fire, and the cabin is lit by paraffin lamps

Below: Toby Toms, a child who has lived all his life on a canal boat. He is wearing a safety harness to stop him falling overboard

Freight

Since water travel is fairly slow, perishable foods, such as dairy produce, meat and fish, are not suitable cargo for inland waterways, unless refrigerated ships can be used. In general, bulk goods, such as timber and metals, are the most usual things transported.

British canal cargoes

The first British canal, the Bridgewater Canal, was built to carry coal. In 1948, when the state took over the canal system, coal was still the most important cargo. Other typical cargoes were timber, metals, liquid fuels and non-perishable food. Much of this was still carried on 25 tonne narrow boats which were loaded and unloaded by hand. By about 1970, commercial traffic on the narrow canals had almost entirely stopped, although over 1,600 kilometres of broader canals and canalized rivers in Britain are still used commercially. About 50,000,000 tonnes of freight are carried each year.

Above: Barges by an Amsterdam quay. The buildings are warehouses

Below: Some modern factories use waterways instead of roads or railways to deliver their products. These push-tows can take as many as 300 Renault cars at a time

Above: Compartment boats are used for carrying coal and other bulk products

This freight is mainly coal, coke, fuel and general merchandise.

Other cargoes

The cargoes carried on inland waterways throughout the world vary according to local needs. Bulk products such as coal, oil, fertilizers, steel, grain, foodstuffs and chemicals are the most important.

Barge-carrying systems

Recently, there has been an important advance in water freight. In Europe and in the USA, barge-carrying systems have been developed so that heavy cargoes can be taken very long distances in the same barges. A number of loaded barges are carried on large sea-going ships. This means that, for example, timber can be moved from the Mississippi all the way to factories in Europe without changing barge. This saves both time and money, since the barges only need to be unloaded once.

BACAT, LASH and SEABEE

There are already three different systems of carrying several barges at the same time. In BACAT (which stands for Barge Aboard Catamaran), up to 10 barges each carrying 147 tonnes can be loaded, as well as 3 LASH lighters. (This system is now rarely used.) LASH ships (LASH stands for Lighter Aboard Ship) carry between 78 and 89 lighters of 380 tonnes each and now operate all over the world. The lighters themselves travel on the major European waterways as part of push-tows. The biggest system of all is the SEABEE system, which can take 38 barges of up to 840 tonnes each. These enormous tonnages are very striking when you compare them with the 25 tonne capacity of the old British narrow boat. You can also see why so many European factories use water transport.

The main canals and waterways of Western Europe and (inset) the canals and waterways of Eastern Europe and part of the Soviet Union

Continuation eastwards

0   750
km

White Sea   •Archangel

FINLAND   *Lake Onega*

Lake Ladoga

•Leningrad

•Kirov

Baltic Sea   •Riga

•Kaliningrad   •Gorky   •Ufa

•Moscow

POLAND   U S S R

•Kiev

Dnepr   •Volgograd

ROMANIA   •Rostov   *Volga*

Danube

Black Sea   *Caspian Sea*

North Sea

Copenhagen•

DENMARK

Baltic Sea   USSR

•Gdansk

UNITED KINGDOM

•Hamburg   •Szczecin

Vistula

THE NETHER–LANDS   •Bremen

Elbe   •Berlin

Amsterdam•

•Warsaw

London•   Rotterdam•

Antwerp•   Duisberg•

Rhine   WEST   EAST   P O L A N D

BELGIUM   GERMANY   GERMANY

English Channel

LUX.   •Prague

•Le Havre   *Seine*   Frankfurt a. Main   CZECHOSLOVAKIA

•Brest   •Paris   •Nuremberg

•Vienna

F   R   A   N   C   E   •Basel   AUSTRIA   •Budapest

Bay of Biscay   SWITZERLAND   HUNGARY

ROMANIA

Lyons•   •Milan   •Venice

Bordeaux•   Belgrade•   *Danube*

Rhône   *Po*

Adriatic Sea   YUGOSLAVIA

I   T   A   L   Y

•Marseilles

S   P   A   I   N   *Mediterranean Sea*   Rome•

Barcelona•

Navigable rivers

Canals

0   300 km

Modern European canals

Since 1945, in both eastern and western Europe, there has been a big programme of canal improvement and extension. Now, inland waterways are among the most important parts of the commercial transport system.

The Trans-Europe Waterway

One good example of this is the Trans-Europe Waterway, which will make it possible to travel across Europe by boat right from the North Sea to the Black Sea. The waterway follows the rivers Rhine, Main and Danube, parts of which have been canalized. By the early 1980's, the whole waterway should be completed. It was opened as far as Nuremburg, which is now an important port, in 1970. This waterway will bring all kinds of benefits. Trade between central Europe and the rest of the world will be made easier.

Canals in the Soviet Union

In the Soviet Union, inland waterways are an essential part of the transport network. The river Volga, which runs for over 3,500 kilometres south through Russia to the Caspian Sea, is the key to the system. From it, waterways have been built to the Baltic, Black Sea and White Sea, and these give Soviet industrial centres direct links with western Europe. The Soviet canal system is also used by traffic travelling from countries such as Germany and Holland to Iran. Boats go via the Kiel Canal in northern Germany to the Baltic and then through the Soviet Union to the Caspian. The route is over 4,000 kilometres shorter than the sea trip through the Suez Canal and therefore saves a great deal of time.

Above: Floating containers can be seen being loaded and unloaded by cargo ships in Rotterdam

Below: Timber being floated along the Volga-Don Canal in the Soviet Union. The logs are fastened together and towed by a boat

Canals in North America

Before the first canals were built in the United States after about 1800, transport to the interior of the country was difficult and slow. It took anything between 18 and 35 days to carry $1-1\frac{1}{2}$ tonnes of goods from Philadelphia to Pittsburgh. By linking the abundant natural waterways—the St Lawrence, Hudson, Ohio, Illinois and Mississippi rivers and the Great Lakes—canals helped to open up the mid-West. This meant that trade could develop and towns could expand.

Above: A huge grain carrier passing through a lock on the Welland Canal

Below: A map showing the St. Lawrence Seaway, the Great Lakes and part of the United States canal system

CANADA

Lake Superior

Duluth

St Lawrence

Ottawa • Montreal

Lake Huron

Lake Michigan

Hudson

Lake Ontario

Detroit • Buffalo • Boston •

Chicago • Lake Erie

Illinois

Pittsburgh

Appalachian Mountains

New York

Philadelphia

St Louis

Ohio

Washington D.C.

Mississippi

U N I T E D

S T A T E S

Atlantic Ocean

Norfolk •

	Navigable rivers
	Canals

300

0   km

Above: A paddle steamer moored on the Mississippi

The Erie Canal

One of the earliest and most important canals was the Erie Canal, started in 1817 and completed after eight years. It ran for 575 kilometres from Albany, a town in New York State on the Hudson River, to Buffalo on Lake Erie. Once it was completed, grain from the rich agricultural lands in the mid-West could be sold in the eastern states, and goods made there and new settlers could easily travel west. New York, which is on the mouth of the Hudson, did very well out of the increased trade.

By 1850, the canal network was 5,600 kilometres long. From then on, faced with competition from the railways, canals became less important. (The one exception was the New York State Barge Canal, which replaced the Erie in 1918.) Rivers, however, never lost their importance.

The Mississippi, which runs for 2,939 kilometres from Minneapolis to New Orleans remains a vital highway for freight. Chicago is a major international port. Before it was connected to the Illinois River (a tributary of the Mississippi) in 1845 by canal, it had been no more than a tiny spot on the map with fewer than 200 inhabitants.

The St Lawrence Seaway

The St Lawrence Seaway is also an important route to the mid-West states. The Seaway was first opened in 1848 and a complete reconstruction was finished in 1959. Now, ocean-going ships can travel inland as far as Duluth on Lake Superior, 3,747 kilometres from the Atlantic, by passing through seven locks. They also sail through the Welland Canal, first built in 1829 and rebuilt and enlarged in 1932.

Suez and Panama

Not all canals were built as part of an inland transport system or to enable seagoing vessels to reach inland ports. Two of the most famous—the Suez Canal and the Panama Canal—were intended to shorten sea routes.

The Suez Canal

Whoever controls the Suez Canal also controls the quickest sea route from Europe to the East. This is why it has been at the centre of international politics ever since it was opened.

The Canal was built by the French engineer Ferdinand de Lesseps and completed in 1869. Seven years later, the British bought it. In 1956, the Egyptian government tried to take it over. French and British troops then invaded it. After two months, they withdrew, and Egypt was left to operate the Canal.

During the 1967 Six-Day War between the Arab nations and Israel, the Canal was closed and blocked. Fifteen ships were trapped there. It was not re-opened until June 1975.

The Canal is 165 kilometres long and 10 metres deep. Its minimum width is 54 metres. It takes about 11 hours to travel through it.

The Panama Canal

The Canal, which is 82 kilometres long, joins the Atlantic and Pacific Oceans and saves shipping a journey of 12,800 kilometres. This means that it is extremely important, from both a military and an economic point of view, especially to the United States.

Its builders ran into every kind of problem. De Lesseps, who built the Suez Canal, was the first to try. His company

Above: The liner *Empress of Britain* passing through one of the locks on the Panama Canal. The ship only just fits

Below: The wrecks of ships sunk during the 1956 Suez War in order to block the Suez Canal

gave up in 1889 after a financial scandal and the death of 22,000 men from yellow fever. In 1904, the United States started again, and 10 years later, on 15 August 1914, the Canal was officially opened.

The Panama locks

Unlike Suez, which has no locks, Panama has three pairs of locks on both the Atlantic and the Pacific sides. They raise and lower vessels 25 metres on their 15 hour journey. Each of the locks is over 333 metres long, though for smaller ships only 133 or 200 metres may be used. There are electric locomotives running on rails on each side of the locks, and these tow boats and ships through.

Since the locks are only 34 metres wide, many modern ships are too wide for them, including the largest tankers and liners and some of the American navy's aircraft carriers. In 1970, a new canal was proposed, to run at sea level through Panama, just north of the Canal Zone.

Above: The Suez Canal and how it joins the Red Sea and the Mediterranean

Below: The Panama Canal and its route across the Gatun Lake. The area inside the white lines is the Canal Zone

The future of inland waterways

It is difficult to talk in a general way about the future of inland waterways. This is because European canals are largely commercial while British canals are not.

Leisure use of canals

In Britain, the narrow boat network, built between 1760 and 1840, is now used chiefly for leisure purposes. Since the early 1960's boating and canoeing on canals have become more and more popular as weekend and holiday activities, especially for children. In 1971, there were nearly 55,000 pleasure craft on British inland waterways. In some areas, derelict locks are now being repaired, so that disused stretches of canal can be reopened for leisure use.

European and American canals

In most countries in Europe and in the United States, inland waterways have a central place in the transport system. This is because the most important routes are suitable for sea-going vessels and a very large amount of freight can be carried at one time. The new barge loading systems mean that canals have become part of international transport routes and will continue each year to become more and more important.

British waterways

Some experts argue that the British government should consider modernizing and widening some of the waterways already built and should also build new ones. This is because waterways can carry heavy freight far more cheaply than lorries, and with much less damage to the countryside and the environment. Lorries however would still have to be used

Above: Children learning how to row on the Regents Canal in London. This has always been busy, once with commercial barges and now with pleasure boats

Below: Repairing and renovating a disused canal in England. It will then be used for boating

for distributing goods to shops and factories. Canals are much quieter than motorways and a lot more pleasant and interesting to look at. Pollution of the air is far less of a problem.

An idea which is being considered at the moment is for a new multi-purpose waterway running from the Wash to the Severn. This canal would run through the industrial areas of central England, and barges of up to 1,500 tonnes and even large push-tows could travel there from abroad by the LASH system. English industrial towns would then be directly linked with the major European ports and industrial areas. Trade with North America would be made simpler. The canal would also act as an enormous water store and distribution system, and would provide new opportunities for boating and holiday-making.

Comparative costs

A canal like this would cost no more to build than a six-lane motorway over the same route, and would be far cheaper to maintain. However, the British government is unlikely to go ahead with the plan. Groups supporting road traffic would probably oppose it strongly, just as canal owners were opposed to the railways in the 19th century. Yet canals, even at their busiest and most modern, have a magic that no motorway could ever have. A major new waterway might well also be very good for British trade.

The canal age in Britain is long since over, and has been replaced by the age of the container lorry. In Europe and the USA inland waterways are, and will continue to be, vital to the economic life of each country in just the same way as motorways and railways.

Above: Brightly painted narrow boats, now used only for holidays

Below: The Princess Irene Sluis in the Netherlands, which is one of the largest economizer locks in Europe. The guillotine gate in the centre shortens the lock when only a few boats use it at one time

BOOKS TO READ

Information about canals
The Shell Book of Inland Waterways, Hugh McKnight; David and Charles, 1975
The Canal Builders, Anthony Burton; Eyre Methuen, 1972
Back Door Britain, Anthony Burton; Andre Deutsch, 1977
Navigable Waterways, L. T. C. Rolt; Longman, 1969
Canals in Towns, Lewis Braithwaite; Adam and Charles Black, 1976
British Canals, Charles Hadfield; David and Charles, 1969
Canal, Anthony Burton, Derek Pratt; David and Charles, 1976
Canals in Colour, Anthony Burton, Derek Pratt; Blandford Press, 1974
Waterways of Western Europe, Hugh McKnight: Guinness Superlatives Ltd 1978
Stories about canals and canal people
Saranne, Violet Bibby; Longman, 1969
Boat Girl, Mary Crockett; Chatto, 1972
Thursday's Child, Noel Streatfield; Armada, 1973
The Canal Children, Brian Wright; Heinemann, 1976

PLACES TO GO

Regent's Canal, London (especially between Paddington and Camden Town)
Bingley staircase locks, *Leeds and Liverpool Canal*
Foxton locks, *Grand Union Canal (Leicester branch)*
Barton Swing Aqueduct, *Bridgewater Canal/ Manchester Ship Canal*
Anderton Lift, *Trent & Mersey Canal/ Weaver navigation*
Lune Aqueduct, *Lancaster Canal*
Pontcysyllte Aqueduct, *Llangollen Canal*
Tardebigge locks, *Worcester & Birmingham Canal*

Waterways Museum, Stoke Bruerne, nr. Towcester, Northampton
Crofton Pumping Station, *Kennet & Avon Canal*
Llangollen Canal Exhibition, Llangollen
National Maritime Museum, Greenwich
Exeter Maritime Museum
Ironbridge Gorge Museum, Telford
Manchester Museum
Camden lock, London (especially *The Pirates' Launch*, which is a centre for children based on an old barge, where rowing is taught).

It is interesting to walk along almost any stretch of canal, whether in town or in the country. Use the gazetteer in the back of *The Shell Book of Inland Waterways* to find out the nearest canals to your home or school. See if you can find old warehouses, wharves, lock-keeper's cottages and old signs put up when narrow boats were still drawn by horses. You can still see marks in some bridges made by the tow-ropes, as well as ramps where horses could be hauled out of the canal if they fell in.

Index

Illustrations appear in
bold type

Amsterdam **34**
Anderton lift **26**, 27
Aqueducts 14, 16, 24-5,
  24-25
Atlantic Ocean 8, 39, 40, 41

BACAT (Barge Aboard
  Catamaran) 35
Barge-carrying systems 35
Barges 17, 22, 29, 30, 32-3,
  32, **33**, **34**
Barton aqueduct 11, **16**, 24,
  25
Belgium 26-7, **27**
Bingley staircase locks **18**
Birmingham 10, 17
Boats **16**, 28-33
  diesel 23, 28, **28**, **31**
  lighters 29, 35
  narrow 28, 30-3, 34, 35,
    43
  on rivers 10, 28
  pleasure 42, **42**
  push-tows 29, **34**, 35
  sea-going 39, 40, **40**, 42
  steam 28, **39**
Bridges 13, **13**
Bridgewater, Duke of 11, **11**
Brindley, James 11, 12, **14**,
  25

Canada see North America
Canal-building 12-15
Canal companies 6-7,
  11-17, 40
Canal life 30-3, **30**, **32**, **33**
Canalization of rivers 6, 8,
  11, 34, 37
Canals:
  Bridgewater 8, 11, **11**,
    12, 24, 34
  Dortmund-Ems 17

Elbe Lateral 27
Erie 39
Grand Union 23
Kiel 37
Latéral à la Garonne 27
Llangollen 24
Manchester Ship **16**, 17,
  25
du Midi 6, 8-9, **8**
New York State Barge 39
Panama 40-1, **40**, **41**
Regents **42**
St Lawrence Seaway **38**,
  39, **40**
Shropshire 26
Suez 37, 40, **40**, **41**
Trans-Europe
  Waterway 37
Trent and Mersey 37
Volga-Don **37**
Wash-Severn
  Waterway 43
Weaver Navigation 27
Welland **7**, **38**, 39
Canal buildings 13, **13**, 33,
  34
Canals, leisure use of **6**, 42,
  42, 43
Canals, state-owned 7, 8-9,
  17, 34
Compartment boats **35**
Contractors 14

Dam 8
Dipper (metal hand-bowl)
  31, 33
Drought 21, **21**
Dutch Barge Dog
  (Keeshond) **30**

Egypt 37, 40
Embankments 14
Engineers 6, 12, **12**, 13, 14
  16, 24, 27
  see also Brindley, Jessop,
  de Lesseps, Riquet,
  Telford
Europe 7, 17, 29, 35, 36-7,
  36, 42, 43

Flights (series of locks) 19
France 6, 8-9, 27, **34**

Gatun Lake **41**
Germany 17, 27, 37
Great Lakes 38, **38**
Guillotine gate on lock, **43**

Hay (inclined plane) 26
Horses, canal **6**, **13**, **16**, 23,
  28, **28**, 30, 33

Inclined plane 26-7, **26**, **27**
Industrial Revolution 6,
  10-11
Ironbridge 26

Jessop, William 13, 24

LASH (Lighter Aboard Ship)
  35, 43
Lake Erie 39
Lake Superior 39
Leggers/legging **22**, 23
Lengthsmen 13
Lesseps, Ferdinand de 40
Lift (instead of lock) **26**,
  27, **27**
Locks 18-19, **18**, **19**, 20,
  21, **21**
  alternatives to 24, 26-7
  derelict, repaired 42
  economizer 19, 43
  electric 41
  European 17, 19, **43**
  guillotine gate **43**
  keeper 13
  on Panama Canal **40**, 41
  staircase 8, 14, **18**, 19
London 17, **42**

Manchester 11, 17
Mediterranean Sea 8, **41**

Narrow boats **43**
Navvies **12**, 15, **15**, 22-3
Netherlands 30, **34**, 37,
  37, **43**

North America 38-39, **38**, **40**, 42, 43; *see also* United States

Panama Canal 40, **40**, 41, **41**
Pacific Ocean 40, 41
Pollution **20**, 21, 42-3
Pontcysyllte Aqueduct 24-5, **24-5**
Pound (stretch of water between locks) 21
Puddling (to make canal beds watertight) 15
Pumping stations 20
Push-tow barges 29, **29**

Railways 6, 7, 11, 16, **16**, **17**, 30, 39, 43
Ramps (for horses) 28
Red Sea **41**
Reservoirs 20, 21
Riquet, Pierre Paul 9
Rivers
    Danube 37
    Dee 24
    Hudson 38, 39
    Illinois 38, 39

Irwell 11
Main 37
Mersey 11
Mississippi 29, 35, 38, 39, **39**
Ohio 38
Rivers 6, 8, **8-9**, 24, 28
    canalized 6, 8, **11**, 34, 37
Rhine 17, **17**, 39
Rhône 17
Saint Lawrence 38
Seine 17
Severn 11, 26, 43
Thames 11
Trent 11
Volga 37
Ronquières 26-7
Roses and castles (boat decorations) 31, **31**
Rotterdam **37**

Saint Lawrence Seaway 38, **38**, 39
SEABEE (barge-carrying system) 35
Ships **7**, 29, 35, 39
Side-ponds (beside locks) 19
Sluice (part of lock) 18

Soviet Union 36-7, **36**
Staircases (series of locks) **18**, 19
Suez Canal 40, **40**, 41
Summit-level (of canal) 20

Tank (part of lift) **26**, 27, **27**
Telford, Thomas 12, **14**, 24
'Token Money' 15
Tolls 13
Tow-path 13, 23, 28, **28**
Troughs (in aqueducts) 24
Tunnels 8, 22-3, **22**, **23**
United States 26, 39, 35, 38-9, **39**, 40, 41
    see also North America

Ventilation shaft (in tunnels) 22-3, **22**

Warehouse 13, **13**
Water 20-1
    can (on barge) **31**
    pollution **20**
    power **26**
    slope 27
Weirs (artificial waterfalls beside locks) 21